OSCAR VISITS VALLEY FORGE

A Dynamic History Adventure

Dedication

To Oscar, a dedicated pug, friend, and who was always there to listen, provide comfort, laughs, and continuous inspiration.

Acknowledgement

I want to thank my wife Holly for always being my rock and for always pushing me to be my better self. You are the love of my life. Also, to my amazing niece Lexi, who provided lots of feedback in helping the adventures of Oscar be even more dynamic!

Dr. Scott receives an invitation to speak about Valley Forge and eagerly accepts, mentioning that his loyal pug, Oscar, will join him! Hearing the news, Oscar perks up, curious about what he will learn. Dr. Scott excitedly shares that Valley Forge was a crucial site during the harsh winter of 1777-1778, where the Continental Army, led by General George Washington, endured great struggles in the fight for independence. He looks forward to touring the historic park and sharing its story with Oscar. As Oscar excitedly dashes around the room, Dr. Scott reminds him that they will leave early and encourages him to dream about the adventures awaiting them.

After quickly doing his morning routine, Oscar watches as Dr. Scott packs his Adventure Bag with all the essentials—blanket, chew toy, food, water, and most importantly, his favorite treat, carrots. Dr. Scott then places an amazing and beautiful American-themed collar featuring a sparkling Liberty Bell around Oscar's neck, hinting at its mysterious historical significance. With their bags packed and excitement in the air, Dr. Scott and Oscar load up into the Freedom Wagon, ready to embark on a DYNAMIC history-filled journey to Valley Forge National Park!

Dr. Scott and Oscar arrive at Valley Forge, where Oscar excitedly explores the replica cabins. Dr. Scott explains their historical significance and reminds Oscar to respect the site. Curious about the past, Oscar rings his special bell, triggering a magical swirl of stars. A young soldier, Joseph Plumb Martin, appears and shares his experiences from 1777-1778. He describes the hardships of winter, cabin building, and the importance of journaling. Oscar listens intently, gaining a new appreciation for history and storytelling.

Oscar, a very curious pug, listens as Martin explains how locals that lived in the area, many known as Quakers, weren't concerned with the war but focused on survival. Martin shares that generals who led the army rented stone homes, while regular soldiers lived in log cabins with dirt floors and no bathrooms. They had to potty outside, sometimes too close to the cabins, causing sanitation issues. Oscar humorously compares this to his own outdoor potty experiences. Martin also mentions how soldiers wore mismatched uniforms due to lack of supplies. Despite the hardships they often endured such as hunger, cold, and disease, the army persevered through the harsh winter encampment.

Dr. Scott calls for Oscar who is still curious about the soldiers' experiences during the harsh winter as Joseph Plumb Martin fades away. Dr. Scott recounts how the soldiers used redoubts and patrols for protection, emphasizing their teamwork and perseverance. As they move on, Oscar, fascinated by the story, is reminded of the importance of working together. Dr. Scott, guiding the tour for Oscar with enthusiasm, shifts their focus to the Memorial Arch, prompting Oscar to wonder aloud what an arch is, eager to learn more.

Oscar, standing in awe before the towering Memorial Arch, exclaims, "Whoa, that thing is huge!" Dr. Scott explains its significance, describing the sacrifices soldiers endured during the harsh winter encampment at Valley Forge. As they walk forward, Oscar's bell jingles, and a sickly man named Jethro appears, sitting beside a tree. Oscar introduces himself and asks, "What is wrong with you?" Jethro, intrigued, shares his story of sickness and the dire conditions surrounding them. Oscar, saddened by the hardship, notes that though many don't appear to be soldiers, everyone seems to be suffering together. Jethro explains that despite the hardships, the people at Valley Forge showed remarkable perseverance, though nearly 2,000 would perish there, with Jethro being the first.

Jethro shares his story with Oscar about the winter encampment during the American Revolution, explaining how people, including over 400 women and children, were brought together by a common cause for personal freedom. Jethro, a freeman, speaks proudly of his journey to fight not only for independence but for equal opportunities for all. Oscar is amazed and asks about the role of women and children, learning they were camp followers who helped with chores, nursed soldiers, and sometimes even spied on the British. Molly Pitcher, a famous camp follower and heroian of the American Revolution, appears and shares how she fought for the revolution after her husband's death. As she fades away, Jethro points out the Memorial Arch, built to honor their sacrifice, and hints at secret rooms at the top, piquing Oscar's curiosity. "Mr. Jethro, I appreciate everything you did! I wish things could have been better for you and everyone here, but I will never forget you," Oscar tells Jethro as he heads back to Dr. Scott and the Freedom Wagon.

As Dr. Scott and Oscar look back at the Memorial Arch, Dr. Scott explains we all have a role to play in remembering the actions of people at Valley Forge as well as making our country a better place today. Oscar knows what Dr. Scott is saying is true, but he sure can't stop wondering what might be hidden in those secret rooms!! Dr. Scott is excited as he tells Oscar it is now time to visit a general with a "mad" personality. Oscar is confused by that, but is excited for the next part of this historical adventure.

Dr. Scott points out General Anthony Wayne to Oscar, explaining his "mad" personality as being someone that would do almost anything for the soldiers he led. Oscar rings his bell, curious about the General's demeanor. General Wayne comes to life and questions Oscar and denies being mad in an exaggerated manner! He explains his intense passion for leading soldiers and how some of his actions, like borrowing cows for instance, were greatly misunderstood. Oscar, puzzled, presses him further, asking about his military history. General Wayne reflects on battles like Brandywine and Germantown, sharing how perseverance led to success at Monmouth, soon after leaving Valley Forge.

General Wayne proudly shares his history with Oscar, recounting his leadership at the Battle of Monmouth and his admiration for General Washington, who later made him the commanding general of the U.S. Army. Oscar, deeply interested in General Wayne's legacy, listens attentively. Dr. Scott, noticing Oscar's admiration for General Wayne, humorously nudges him to say goodbye to the statue of General Wayne, playfully asking him to remind the general not to take any more cows, referencing the past, funny incident.

Oscar, with a smile, complies and playfully delivers the message as he prances back to the Freedom Wagon. Noticing Dr. Scott's excitement, Oscar looks up at Dr. Scott, wondering what could be next. Dr. Scott, with energy in his voice, lets Oscar know their dynamic history adventure is going to continue by learning about the great Prussian general with a BIG personality. Oscar wonders who that could be, but is excited to find out.

Oscar and Dr. Scott stand on the Grand Parade field, where Dr. Scott explains how General Baron Von Steuben trained colonial soldiers as he reads a placard. Oscar, intrigued but confused, asks about the training process. Dr. Scott tells Oscar that General Von Steuben was famous for saying, "Where he came from, all he had to do was tell soldiers what to do and they would do it. However, in America, he had to explain to soldiers why they had to do something and then they would do it." Oscar knew he wanted to learn more, so as Dr. Scott wanders off, he wiggles his Liberty Bell and General Von Steuben comes to life! Von Steuben, in a grand tone, explained that instead of food, he fed the soldiers knowledge and discipline through repetitive drills. Oscar, still puzzled, questions how the soldiers learned this. A smile crosses General Von Steuben's face as he feels the need to show Oscar how the drills were done!

General Von Steuben swoops Oscar up and has him get with the other soldiers. Looking curiously now at Oscar, Von Steuben, in a grand tone, explains that he developed discipline in the soldiers through repetitive drills. There would be marching, learning how to load and fire a musket properly, and ways for soldiers to defend themselves. Von Steuben says the best way to learn is through experience. "Oscar, you are now part of the Continental Army. Hence, let the training begin." A surprised look crosses Oscar's face as he realizes he is now training to be a soldier!

Von Steuben trains Oscar through drills, emphasizing practice, teamwork, and paying attention. Oscar, tired but inspired, learns about the hardships soldiers endured for freedom. Von Steuben explains, while the soldiers march, how Americans had unity of a common cause during the American Revolution, despite many differences. Oscar reflects on how people today argue, and sometimes yell at one another, instead of working together. Von Steuben shares his belief in America's strength through unity, belief in a higher cause, and having the spirit to overcome obstacles. Oscar, moved, recognizes the greatness of his country and the importance of never giving up. Everyone plays a role in his or her country succeeding.

Oscar and General Von Steuben look out over the Grand Parade as soldiers train in the distance. Oscar with a sad expression, softly says, "I am not sure things like this can happen now because it seems like everyone never gets along." Von Steuben, bending down to gently rub Oscar's ear, responds with great wisdom, "Never underestimate the American spirit my little friend. Just like the mist on the field out there, the American spirit is always with us. Sometimes it is hard to see, and sometimes it seems like it is fading, but it is always there." As Oscar contemplates what General Von Steuben just said, he hears Dr. Scott calling for him. Oscar says bye to the Prussian general with the "BIG" personality and runs off, excited about what is next on this dynamic historical adventure.

As Dr. Scott starts explaining about General James Mitchell Varnum's leadership at Valley Forge, Oscar wanders off ringing his bell and runs into the leg of a very determined looking man. "You must be General Varnum," Oscar says. "Yes, I am and you must have just come from visiting the great General Von Steuben." General Varnum explains his soldiers are training with techniques learned from Von Steuben and we should all be grateful General Von Steuben immigrated to America to help us win the American Revolution. General Varnum tells Oscar that even though the men he led were very diverse in terms of background, race, and language, he did not have anyone quite like the pup in front of him.

General Varnum tells Oscar that many people in his time were treated unfairly due to differences like skin color and beliefs, but he believed everyone was important and could make a difference when given a chance. Oscar didn't like people treating others badly just because they may look different and neither did General Varnum. Throughout the time at Valley Forge, General Varnum would meet with George Washington to discuss how all types of soldiers could make a difference. Overtime, George Washington adapted his views and allowed black soldiers to serve at Valley Forge. General Varnum was proud that he was referred to as the "light of the encampment" because of his wise views on unity and how he emphasized that everyone, even people like General Washington, can grow, change, and become even better leaders. With that, Oscar says goodbye to the wise General Varnum and heads back to Dr. Scott, thinking about how we are all important to the American cause.

Oscar and Dr. Scott arrives at the beautiful Washington Memorial Chapel and notices an awesome looking bell on the inside. Dr. Scott explains the bell is a replica of the Liberty Bell, like the one hanging from Oscar's collar. Many years ago, women didn't have a right to vote and an amazing lady named Katharine Wentworth Ruschenberger raised money to create this bell, known as the Justice Bell. Then it was put on the back of a pickup truck to encourage people to support the right to vote for all women. Oscar thought everyone could vote, but maybe at one time they couldn't. "Is that the reason the bell is here at Valley Forge?" Oscar pondered as he looked at the bell. Oscar even thought that maybe George Washington and his troops guarded this bell.

Oscar, being very curious about all this walks into the room the bell was housed, wiggling his own bell. Suddenly a lady appears from behind the Justice Bell, waving and smiling at him.

"Wow! Are you Ms. Ruschenberger?" Oscar asks the lady. "Yes, I am and thank you for visiting the Justice Bell." Ruschenberger explains after all the work to get women the right to vote, the 19th Amendment was passed. Then, sadly, no one wanted the Justice Bell. However, soon the Washington Memorial Chapel, right here in Valley Forge, decided the bell could be here and it has been ever since. Oscar, still curious about how the bell connects to what else he has been learning, wants to know if George Washington guarded the bell?

Ruschenberger laughs and
says the story of the Justice Bell happened long
after General Washington was here, but Valley
Forge is the perfect location for it because the
story of the winter encampment and the Justice
Bell both involved perseverance, overcoming
obstacles, fighting for a common cause, and
represents what is best about the American spirit.
Oscar, feeling inspired, hears Dr. Scott yelling
it is time to go see General Washington's
headquarters! Saying goodbye, Oscar sprints out!

As Dr. Scott and Oscar arrive at the headquarters
of George Washington, Dr. Scott covers
Oscar's eyes with a red, white, and blue cloth.
"Oscar, when I take this cloth off, you are going
to see an amazing place that was very special here
at Valley Forge," Dr. Scott tells Oscar.
Eager and wagging his tail, Oscar anxiously waits.
When the cloth is removed, Oscar gasps in
awe at General Washington's winter headquarters
during the encampment. As Oscar is set
down, he runs excitedly toward the front, ringing
his bell. Oscar can't wait to hopefully meet
General Washington! Seeing Oscar go wild, Dr.
Scott is thrilled at how Oscar is loving all the
history about Valley Forge.

Oscar slides to a screeching halt as he sees boots in front of him and looks up at a giant man in uniform. "Oscar asks, "Are you GENERAL GEORGE WASHINGTON?" "I am and I welcome you to my headquarters. You are at a very special place." Oscar, after giving his name, excitedly tells General Washington that he has met many amazing people during his visit, but wants to really understand why he should always remember what happened here. "Oscar, my little friend, this very important place is where the American spirit grew stronger and where, at seemingly one of our darkest moments, we came together and survived not only tough conditions here, but our own doubts of winning the American Revolution. Here at Valley Forge, men, women, and children, all played a role in making sure that we survived the winter, became more resilient, and became stronger in our belief that the fight for liberty, freedom, and opportunity is worth the effort. Sit here with me on this step," Washington says as he bends down to pick Oscar up.

Discussing courage and perseverance with General Washington, Oscar asks, "So, was everything perfect when you and the army left Valley Forge?" Washington, smiles wearily and says, "No Oscar, it wasn't. Just like life in your time, there was a lot of change, growth, and understanding we still needed to do when we left this amazing place, including me. Always remember Oscar, what makes America special is not that it is perfect, but we have a country that allows everyone to grow, change, better themselves, and follow their dreams. As a country and people, we should always strive for excellence." Oscar tells General Washington that Dr. Scott tells him to always finish strong. Oscar imagines what General Washington just told him is kind of like that.

"Yes Oscar, it is. Keep doing your best, use your time wisely, and be respectful to everyone. Just like I have always done with the soldiers I led, I believe in you and know once you leave here, you will succeed in whatever you do. Perseverance and a positive spirit have done wonders in all ages." Hearing Dr. Scott calling out that it was time to go, and knowing the dynamic adventure was almost over, Oscar tells General Washington it was wonderful meeting him. "General Washington, I will never forget this day and how much I learned. If you and the Continental Army can persevere at Valley Forge during tough times, then I can get through things as well."

Washington, happy to hear this, tells Oscar, "Remember these words: keep working with everyone to strengthen the American foundation so that all people can build a life of success. That may be a little confusing, but people and pups have more in common than we differ over." Finally, General Washington emphasizes, "Focus on how you can connect with others and continue to live a life in a way that will always make a positive impact. Farewell my little friend," Washington says as Oscar runs ahead to Dr. Scott and the Freedom Wagon!

What a day of dynamic learning Oscar! It is almost like everything around here came alive," Dr. Scott says as he winks at Oscar. Dr. Scott then tells Oscar it is time to go speak to a lot of students and get them excited about Valley Forge. Dr. Scott reaches into the Adventure backpack and tells Oscar for being such a good little buddy today, he gets two treats! Oscar eagerly takes each carrot, crunches them, and of course, wishes he had more. Oscar prances, smiles, and looks back to see "Mad" Anthony Wayne, Jethro, Molly Pitcher, General Von Steuben, and others, all waving goodbye. Oscar knows he will never forget VALLEY FORGE!

About the Author

Dr. Scott is an acclaimed educational leader who has earned numerous honors throughout his career. Dr. Scott has taught U.S. History at every level and studied multidisciplinary education at the University of Tennessee-Chattanooga and later, received his Ph.D. in leadership from the University of Alabama. The journey to write this adventure began after obsessing over the need for young students to fully understand and appreciate their history. When Dr. Scott is not writing, he can be found exercising, reading, or exploring the beautiful landscape of the United States. He is passionate about the United States and helping kids learn the full history of this great country in a dynamic way! Dr. Scott loves visiting schools to provide presentations, workshops, and keynote talks.

The End